Published by
Adventuresome Words
Northumberland
England
www.adventuresomewords.co.uk
info@adventuresomewords.co.uk

First published by Adventuresome Words in 2023.
Text and illustrations copyright © Dr K. P. George (pen name for Dr Kassi Psifogeorgou) 2023.
Illustrator: Laura Mocelin.

All rights reserved. This book or parts thereof may not be reproduced in any form, stored in any retrieval system, or transmitted in any form by any means; electronic, mechanical, photocopy, recording, or otherwise, without prior written permission of the publisher.

Dr K. P. George
The Wicked Turnip in Christmas Foodland: A rhyming Christmas story
ISBN: 978-1-7384405-0-4

2nd edition

To Mum and Dad for teaching us the true meaning of Christmas and for bringing magic to our home.

To my sister, for sharing all the magic moments of our youth.

To the family I made, the four angels in my life.

In "Mr Pizza Makes Friends," Mr Pizza felt really sad,
Wicked Turnip was mean at a party, and that was bad.

His best friend, Mr Spinach, so nice and smart,
Asked everyone to help and give Mr Pizza a new start.

They thought and thought until they found a great way,
To make Mr Pizza happy and keep the sadness away.

It worked! Mr Pizza smiled, feeling so good,
He knew he belonged, just like everyone should.

But now, it's Christmas time, and guess who's here with a frown?
It's Wicked Turnip again, trying to bring Pizza down.

"Jingle bells, I hear them ring,
But to me, it's just the same old thing.

'Be kind, be nice,' that's what they sing,
But I'd rather play and be the mischief king!"

In Foodland's streets, so much FUN,
Lights and magic for everyone!

Now Pizza's cool, a star so bright,
Changed for good, he's pure delight.

"Hey, Mr Pizza, will you light up the tree?"
Mrs Carrot smiled, as happy as could be.

"I'd love to! It's lots of fun, as you will soon see!
Little Carrots, want to join me? It's easy as one, two, three!"

"YES, YES, YES," they all shouted with joy,
So happy and excited, every girl and boy!

In the town's heart, by the tree,
The tables are set for you and me.

"Miss Egg, wow, you've done so great,
Chocolate fountains? Can't wait!

"'Take a sip,' she laughed with cheer,
You helped a lot, my dear Spinach, here!

Sweets and gifts, under the tree,
A perfect Christmas, wait and see!

In Foodland, filled with laughter and play,
Secret Santa time is here today!

Pick a name and SHHHH... it's a secret game,
To give a gift and spread joy; it's never the same!"

Whom you'll surprise, just you know,
In our little game, big smiles will surely grow!

Back in the square, Mayor Cauliflower gives a cheer,
Through the magic orb, Mrs Claus is here!

"What's that orb?" the little Carrot asked with a stare,
"It shines so bright!" in the crisp, chilly air.

"It's magic, dear, with a shiny light,
Connects us to Santa's special night!

You see, we help the elves with toys so grand,
For kids in every single land."

"Remember the smell when Christmas day does begin?"
Mum said with a smile, her warmth shining within.

"Christmas magic it starts from deep in our heart,
Then Santa's bag shares it, like a work of art!"

"Really? Wow, that's so cool, Mum!"
Little Carrot grinned, ready to hum.

"I'll tell my friends. They should know,
Our Christmas magic, it's not just for show!"

WOO HOO! the foods all shout.

"We love you Mrs Claus, there's no doubt!

With a screech and a vroom, what's that you hear?
A shiny car came, and Turnip was near!

Mrs Olive whispered, "Oh no, not on this special day,
Poor Mr Pizza, what will he say?'

CREEEEEEEEE

"Hey friends, look who's here to play,
It's me, Turnip, with my cheeky say!

Don't worry, all, I'll make things fun,
Pizza's dull time is now done!

Hey, Mr Mayor, look and see,
I'm the best choice for lighting the tree."

The lights were low, Turnip couldn't see,
Pizza's changed, happy as can be.

He thought he'd poke, and he thought he'd prod,
But everyone's united, strong, not flawed.

Mr Pizza smiled oh so wide,
Kindness in his eyes, he couldn't hide.

"Hey, Turnip, buddy, you're here too!
Let's light this tree, just me and you."

Turnip gawked, eyes popped in shock,
Mr Pizza's change, a real knock.

"Green moustache? Really?" he said,
But Pizza smiled, no hint of dread.

He stepped closer, one, two, three,
"Stop right there!" yelled Turnip, let me be!

But Pizza hugged him oh so tight,
The crowd clapped and laughed, oh, what a sight!

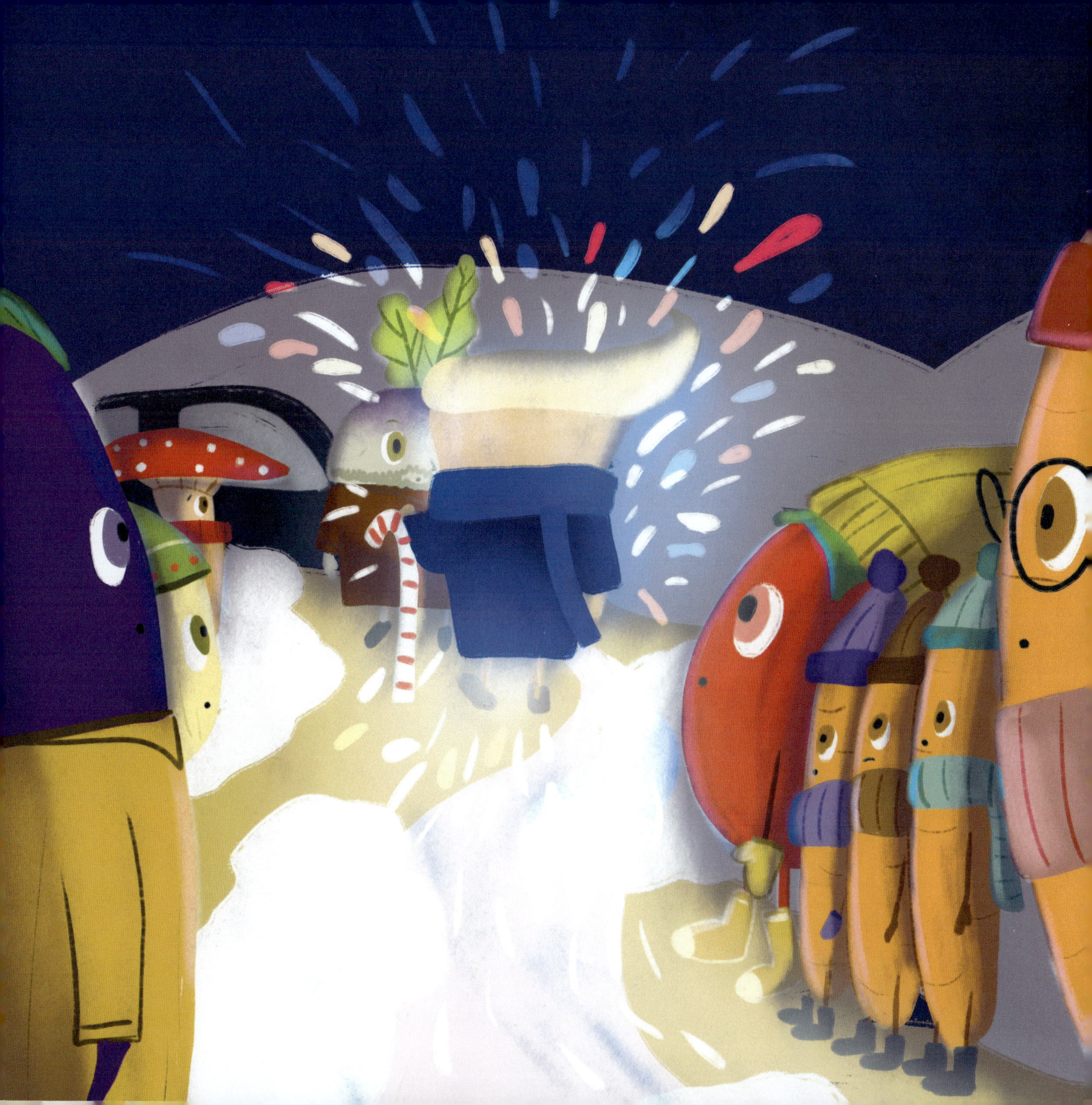

In magic's twirl, colours so bright,
Turnip and Pizza took flight that night!

With love and light, they made a change,
Turnip learned kindness; it's really strange!

And then he felt tears; he let them flow free,
" Being kind is COOL; it's the way to be!"

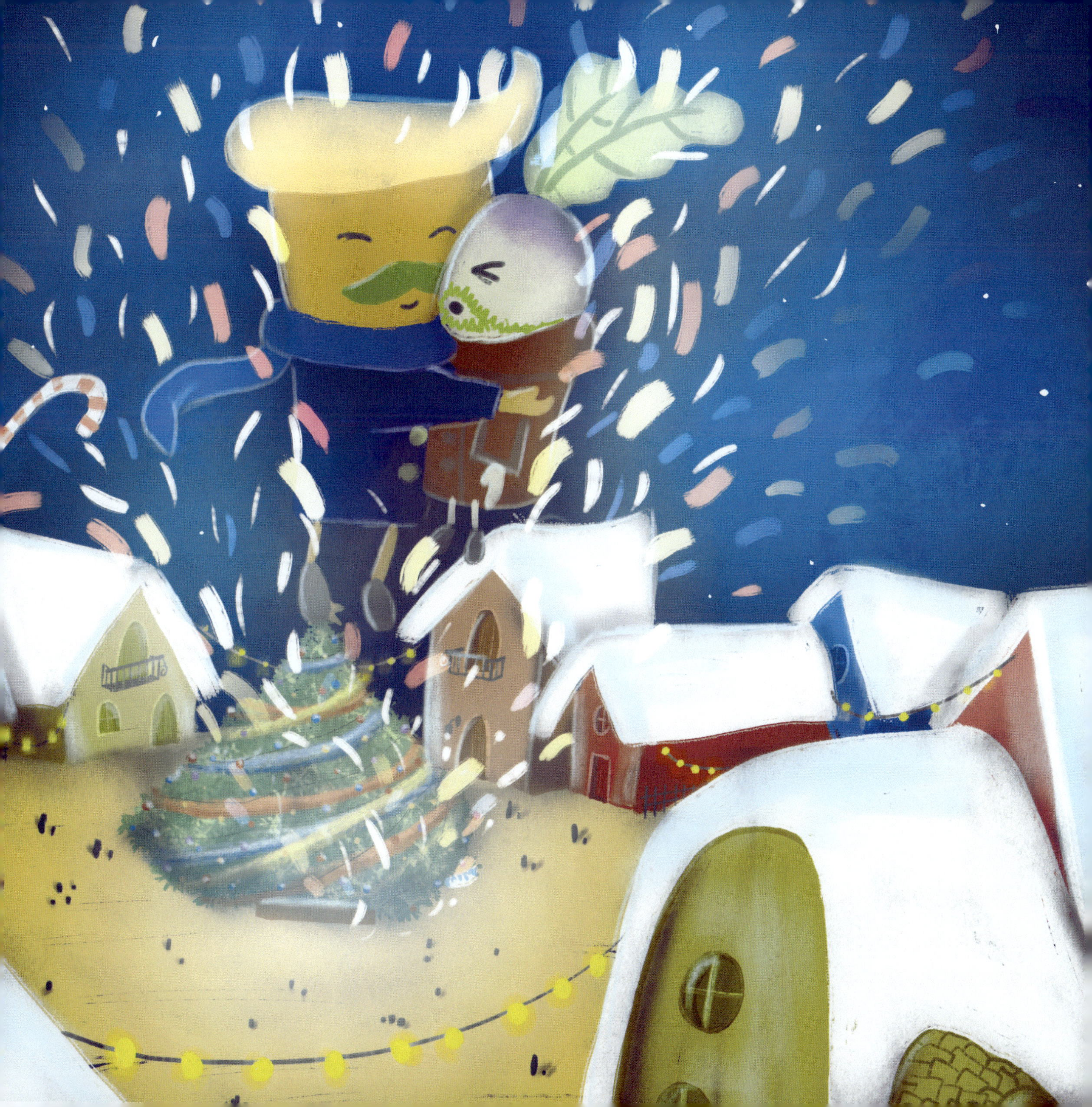

Bells rang out, a sign so fine,
Santa's here to spread joy right on time.

"Santa, you came!" they all cheered so proud,
Full of joy, in a happy crowd.

"I can't stay much," he said so light,
Gotta go on this busy night.

But, before I'm out of sight,
I want to see your tree all lit up and bright!"

"Hey, Turnip and little carrots, come quick,
It's time to light the tree. Give that switch a flick!"

"Let's count," cheered the mayor, happy and loud,
"10 to 1, come on crowd!"

"10, 9, 8," they all shouted with glee,
"7, 6, 5, 4," as happy as could be.

"3, 2, 1," voices so loud and strong,
"Flick the switch, you can't go wrong!"

Lights and baubles, shining so bold,
It looked like Santa's home if truth be told.

"Happy holidays!" cheered all the food,
With hugs and kisses, in a happy mood.

Around the tree, they began to sing,
Carols of joy, let the Christmas bells ring!

"Deck the Halls" and "Jingle Bells" filled the air,
"O' Christmas Tree" ended the songs with flair!

"Is this the best, or could there be more?"
Pizza asked Turnip, feeling happy at his core.

"No, this is it, you've made me see,
Kindness and love is the way to be."

Be part of the story

Imagine you're one of the triplet carrots. How would you feel when you see Turnip change?

What makes Mr Pizza special? Why do you think he chose to share his magic with Turnip, despite his past behaviour?

Be kind like Santa and make people happy this Christmas. Can you do ten nice things? Like giving clothes you don't wear to those who need them. Or writing a letter to someone you love, telling them how much you care. You can also sit with a friend you don't usually sit with at lunch to make them feel special.

Tag Kassi on Social Media.
She would love to hear from you!

🌐 www.adventuresomewords.com
✉️ drkassi@adventuresomewords.com
📷 @drkassi
📘 @authorkassipsifogeorgou

About the Author

Dr Kassi Psifogeorgou, using the pen name Dr K.P.George, grew up in Greece, where she spent most of her youth playing outside and swimming in the sea with her friends.

For as long as she can remember, Kassi has always wanted to be a scientist and a writer. She's an expert in cell and molecular biology, with a master's in biotechnology and a second master's and a PhD in neuroscience.

She writes on culture, kindness, teamwork, and cheering on yourself to be who you are. Her books have been chosen as the books of the month at schools and have sparked conversations about important issues for young people who read them.

"Our Very Greek Easter" received two literary awards and became a best-seller within 3 days of publishing.

'Through my books, I wish to inspire more young people to cultivate a resilient mindset, raise awareness of different cultures and important issues, and engage more children with the fascinating world of science.'

Kassi lives in England with her husband and their three children.

The Wicked Turnip in Christmas Foodland

Follow Laura on Social Media.
       She would love to hear from you!

@ @lauramocelinart

@ @laauramocelin

✉ contato@lauramocelin.com

About the Illustrator

I'm Laura Mocelin, illustrator and architect living in the north of Rio Grande do Sul, Brasil. I was born in 1996 in Santa Catarina and since then I introduced art in my life in many different ways.

My graduation in architecture and urbanism helped a lot to develop myself as an artist, especially regarding to space, time and dimensions. I always liked to draw on paper, with paint and brushes. But digital art won my heart due to the immense amount of possibilities it gives artists, besides allowing for a more in depth study of light, color and stroke. Today I illustrate mainly children's books, which take me back to my childhood and make me see life in a different way.

You Might Also Like

Mr Pizza Makes Friends

*** When the mean Turnip starts teasing Mr Pizza, he starts feeling really down and wonders if he's good at making friends. But in the awesome world of Foodland, there are kind food friends who are always ready to help with a bit of magic! ***

On Amazon

"Mr Pizza Makes Friends" will speak to any kid working up the nerve to open up and make friends at school. A book about self-appreciation, persistence, and ultimately cheering on our friends to be who they are.

You Might Also Like

On Amazon a

Our Very Greek Easter: A very Orthodox Easter
STORY MONSTERS APPROVED

*** Tom's family is flying to Greece for Easter to visit Yiayia, Papou and the rest of their extended family. He's so excited to get acquainted with all the Greek traditions of the Holy Week. So, he writes a letter to his best friend describing what he and his brothers did every day, starting from Lazarus Saturday to Easter Sunday.***

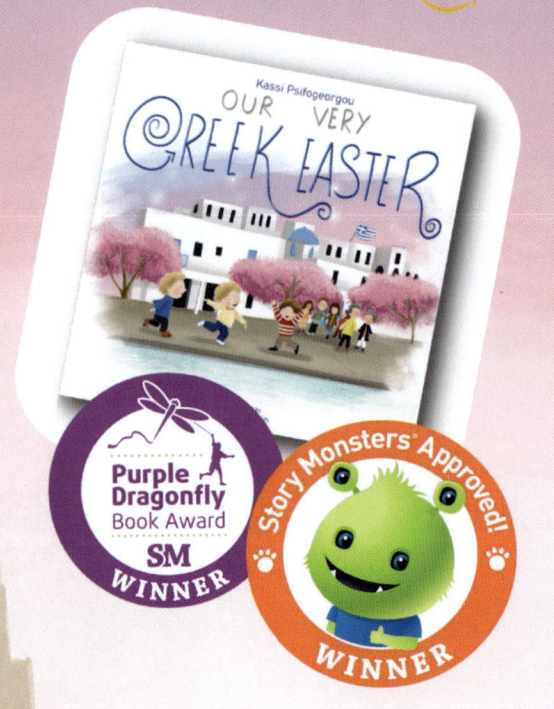

Travel to Greece through this gorgeously illustrated book and learn about the Holy Week in Greek Culture from a Christian perspective. Read about the wonderful traditions that still carry on and the delicious Greek meals planned for the special days!

This book is a keepsake gift that children can enjoy all over the world, focused on the Greek Orthodox Easter.

Our Very Greek Summer: And a very Greek Baptism

Alina and her mom have been invited to a baptism in Greece over the summer by their close friends, the Papadopoulos family.

Get ready for an enchanting journey through this stunningly illustrated story, and read about world-famous Greek hospitality! Learn about a traditional Greek baptism, from the godparents' important role to the celebratory feast and dancing called "gledi".

This book is a keepsake gift that children can enjoy all over the world, focused on the Greek 'philoxenia' and the Greek Orthodox Baptism.

On Amazon a

Printed in Great Britain
by Amazon